Introduction

Information and skills you will acquire

Developing Interview Skills is one of a valuable and user-friendly new series of easy-to-read booklets created specially to help you develop at work. The materials have been created from actual experience in workplace training. Experts from Workbase Training and Campaign for Learning have pooled their knowledge and experience to involve you in learning new skills and building on those you already have. This booklet is divided into clear sections, containing specially devised *activities* and a *mini project*, to allow you to practise as you learn.

Developing Interview Skills will enable you to:

- [ ] Understand the aims of the interview and the interview process.

- [ ] Prepare effectively for the interview.

- [ ] Put across the right information and image during the interview.

- [ ] Review performance and experiences after the interview.

Getting the most out of this booklet

- [ ] You may want to work through the booklet from start to finish or focus on an area of interest.

- [ ] Once you have completed the questionnaire on page 4, you will be able to see clearly which topics you need most help with, and which areas you can safely leave out.

- [ ] The questionnaire will also allow you to create your own learning plan, for which an example and space is provided on page 5.

- [ ] You may want to ask your supervisor or another colleague for their views on the areas you could work on, or for help with the activities in the booklet.

- [ ] As you may want to use the booklet for future reference, you may want to write the answers out in rough first and then write them in the booklet.

Questionnaire

What do you need most help with?

This questionnaire is to enable you to think about what interview skills you need most help with.
Tick the boxes as appropriate.

	1	2	3
	I need a lot of help	**I need some help**	**I can cope**
SECTION 1: Understanding what an interview is			
Completing the application form			
SECTION 2: Preparing answers to possible questions			
Checking my appearance			
SECTION 3: Knowing what to expect at the interview			
Responding to different types of questions			
SECTION 4: Reviewing my performance after the interview			
Making sure that I do not make the same mistakes next time			

The most important areas for you to concentrate on are those which you have marked 1 or 2.

DEVELOPING INTERVIEW SKILLS. LEARNING FOR WORK Series. © Workbase Training

Create your own learning plan

Example: My learning plan for developing interview skills.

I need to go through the following areas to make sure that I am getting them right:

1. Understanding what an interview is (Section 1)

2. Reviewing my performance after the interview (Section 4)

I need to increase my confidence and spend the most time on this area:

3. My performance during the interview (Section 3)

Write your own learning plan here. The questionnaire on page 4 will help you get started.

_____

_____

_____

_____

_____

_____

_____

_____

_____

_____

_____

_____

_____

_____

_____

_____

_____

_____

Section 1 UNDERSTANDING WHAT AN INTERVIEW IS

What is an interview?

An interview is an opportunity for you to demonstrate face to face that you have the necessary skills, experience and knowledge to perform, for example, a particular role or job successfully.

Interviews may apply to different situations. These might include:

- job interviews
- interviews for promotion
- an application to join a club or organisation.

The interviewer will be looking for answers which indicate that you can meet the criteria or requirements of the role or job so that you would be able to carry out the job effectively.

Different jobs will have particular requirements. For example, possible requirements might be:

- experience of caring for the elderly
- a basic knowledge of motor mechanics.

At the interview you can expect to be asked whether you are able to meet the relevant requirements.

In order to prove that you are the best candidate for the job, your preparation will begin when you first decide to apply for the job.

The recruitment process

This begins with an advertisement of some sort, whether in a shop window or, more usually, in a newspaper or trade journal. Adverts vary, but generally people are asked to respond by telephoning for an application form or sending a 'Curriculum Vitae' (C.V.), which is a list of a person's skills and experience.

Once you have completed and returned your application form or C.V., the recruiters will assess whether or not you have the right skills, experience and knowledge that they are looking for. If they think that you may be suitable, they will ask you to attend an interview in order to find out in more detail about your possible aptitude for the job.

The application form and other materials

The application form varies from one organisation to another. Larger organisations will probably have more formal procedures. As well as an application form, they may also send you information about the main duties of the job and the level of skills, experience and knowledge they are looking for. These requirements are often referred to as the person specification or job criteria.

You will need to read through all the information very carefully. Draft out your answers in rough first of all and try to make sure that your answers demonstrate that you can meet the criteria for the job.

Example: The criteria may include experience of retail work.

Answer: For the last five years I have worked part-time as a sales assistant for Tesco. My duties include: customer service, handling returned goods and queries, checking out goods and cash handling.

Activity 1

Think about your current job, either paid or voluntary, or one which you have had previously.

What levels of skills, experience and knowledge do you think are necessary for effective performance?

List 4 points.

_____

_____

_____

_____

You will find the feedback to this activity on page 22.

What does an interview involve?

Interviews normally follow a certain format. For example, a job interview may take the following format:

- You are taken to the interview room.
- You are greeted and introduced to the interviewer(s) and asked to sit down.
- The interviewer may chat informally with you for a few minutes to break the ice.
- The interviewer may briefly talk to you about the job and the organisation.

- You are asked questions to give you the opportunity to demonstrate that you are the most suitable candidate for the job.
- You are given the opportunity to ask questions about the job and the organisation.
- The interviewer thanks you for attending the interview and tells you how and when they will be getting in touch with you.

Activity 2

Raja is looking for a job. He sees an advertisement in the paper for an assistant at a local tyre-fitting company. He rings up and asks for an application form. When it arrives he asks his sister to complete it for him because he cannot be bothered with such things.

He is asked to attend an interview. The interviewer asks questions relating to the form and Raja bluffs his way through them because he is not clear about what is on the form. He doesn't get the job. Advise Raja on how he should have prepared for the interview.

_____

_____

_____

_____

_____

_____

You will find the feedback to this activity on page 22.

Key Learning Points

☐ When applying for a job, read through all of the information that you are sent very carefully.

☐ Follow all of the instructions that are given on the application form.

☐ Ask someone to help you complete the application form if you have any difficulty.

☐ Write out your answers in rough first of all.

☐ Make sure you demonstrate that you meet all of the requirements for the job.

DEVELOPING INTERVIEW SKILLS. LEARNING FOR WORK Series. © Workbase Training

Section 2   PREPARING YOURSELF FOR THE INTERVIEW

The first steps in your preparation

If you are invited for an interview, this means that the recruiters think that you may be a suitable candidate for the job. What you need to do now is to build on the skills and experience that you have written about in your application form or C.V., in order to prove that you are the best candidate for the job.

Start by reading through your completed application form and all the other materials very carefully, so that you are clear about what the organisation is looking for.

Questions you may be asked

Look at the person specification or job criteria and think about likely questions that you might be asked. Below are some examples.

Q. Tell me about your current job.

Try to emphasise those skills which are also needed for the job for which you have applied.

For example, if your current job is a cleaner at a leisure centre and you are applying for a job as a home carer, you would emphasise the domestic skills that you use, such as hoovering and polishing, as well as the more general skills, such as teamworking and completing paperwork.

Q. Why do you want the job?

Be sure about your reasons for wanting the job. Talk about things that interest you about it and what you enjoy. Avoid referring to money and holidays. Do not give negative reasons such as being fed up with your current job and do not run down your current job or employer.

Q. What interests you about the job?

Try to be clear about this. The interviewer will want to know that you are motivated enough to perform the job effectively. You could mention the environment or your interest in meeting people, for example.

'I've always been interested in leisure.'
'I enjoy meeting a wide variety of people and helping them out.'

Q. What are your strengths and weaknesses?

Try to emphasise the strengths that are needed for the job. For example:

- accuracy with figures
- thoroughness
- paying attention to detail
- energy
- getting on well with people
- being a good teamworker
- experience of this type of work.

When talking about your weaknesses, try not to put the interviewer off you by being too honest! You could try to mention something which could also be a strength in some circumstances. For example:
  'I find it difficult to switch off from work sometimes.'
  'I take my job very seriously.'

Q. What skills and qualities could you bring to the job?

Think about those skills that the job requires. For example, they might include cash handling, cleaning, production line work, electronic assembly.

You will also need to think about the more general skills that an interviewer may be looking for. These might include:

- being a good team worker
- accuracy
- problem solving
- getting on with other people
- keeping calm under pressure.

Situational questions

As well as the types of question listed above, you may also be asked questions which test how you would react in a particular situation. For example:
  'What would you do if an angry customer returned goods and demanded a refund?'
  'What would you do if the machine you were working on broke down?'

What will you wear?

As part of your interview preparation, you need to think about the way you will dress. Your choice of clothes can show that you have taken the trouble to look smart and dressed appropriately for the occasion.

For men, a white shirt, a subtle tie and a darkish suit are the most suitable clothes to wear for office-based and retailing jobs. For women, a smart jacket and skirt in a non-bright colour and a formal blouse are the best choice. Smart trouser suits are also acceptable to most employers.

In jobs where more casual or protective clothing is worn, then smart trousers, a jacket and shirt and perhaps a tie are the customary clothing for men. For non-office based jobs or where protective clothing is worn, a smart skirt, blouse and cardigan are acceptable for women.

You also need to ensure that your hair is neat and tidy. Try to be sensitive to the type of organisation that you are visiting. In some organisations, for instance, large earrings would be perfectly acceptable, while in others this might not fit in with their image.

For jobs requiring food handling, be extra sure that you appear clean and tidy.

If you are being recruited through an agency, take their advice on what should be worn for an interview.

How will you get there?

To be sure of arriving in good time, you will need to consider in advance your route and mode of transport and be clear about where exactly the interview will be held. Work out roughly how long it will take you to get there. Allow yourself extra time in case of delays (at least 20 minutes, or more if you have to travel any distance).

You will probably have been sent a map when you were asked to attend for interview, but if you aren't sure how to find the place you should telephone the organisation and ask for directions and, if necessary, details of the nearest bus stop or tube station.

If you are not familiar with the area take a map with you.

Activity 3

If you were being interviewed for your current or most recent job, how would you answer the following questions? (If you have an interview coming up, use this exercise as part of the preparation for that instead of basing it on your current or most recent job.)

Q. Tell me about your current job.

Q. Why do you want the job?

Q. What interests you about the job?

Q. What are your strengths and weaknesses?

FEEDBACK: Ask a friend or colleague to go through your answers with you.

Q. What skills and qualities could you bring to the job?

Write down your answers on a separate sheet of paper.

Activity 4

Bernie will shortly be attending an interview for a job as a checkout assistant at a supermarket in a neighbouring town. He is very keen to get the job. Give him some advice about what he can do to prepare himself for the interview.

_____

_____

_____

_____

You will find the feedback to this activity on page 22.

Key Learning Points

☐ Start your preparation for the interview by reading through the application form and other materials very carefully.

☐ Be clear about what skills, knowledge and experience you have, particularly those which are relevant to the job.

☐ Think about the requirements of the job and jot down answers to questions that you may be asked at the interview.

☐ Consider in advance what you are going to wear.

☐ Find out where the interview is being held and work out how long it will take you to get there.

Section 3 KNOWING WHAT TO EXPECT AT THE INTERVIEW

What happens at an interview

You will be asked to attend the interview at a specific time and place. When you arrive, follow whatever instructions you are given, such as reporting to the reception desk, or asking the receptionist to ring a number to let the appropriate person know you have arrived. Give yourself enough time to relax before you are called in to the interview.

Usually someone will come and collect you and take you to the interview room. Always be polite and friendly to everyone you meet, as these people are sometimes asked how they got on with you.

At the start

When you are taken into the interview room, respond according to the way you are greeted. If the interviewer says 'Good morning' you should do the same, or if they say 'Hello' then answer in the same way. Normally the person or people interviewing will start off with some friendly chat to make you feel relaxed.

Questions

Sometimes the interviewer will begin by telling you about the job. Alternatively, they may go straight to the questions. At the end of the interview, you will usually be given an opportunity to ask any questions. Try to think of something in advance that you want to know about the job, but make sure that the question has not already been covered. It is all right to ask questions about the terms and conditions of the job, but try not to make it seem as if these are your main interest.

At the end

At the end of the interview, it is usual for the interviewer to tell you what will happen next – that is, they will write or telephone to let you know whether or not you have been successful. If the interviewer does not tell you about this, then you can ask.

When the interview is over, thank the interviewer for seeing you, say 'Goodbye' and leave the interview room.

Dos and don'ts at the interview

Do:
- give yourself time to think about your answers and try not to say just the first thing that comes into your head
- try to be friendly and not abrupt
- relax and talk to the interviewer as you would to any other human being
- talk about your skills and achievements and don't be afraid to blow your own trumpet
- if you feel yourself tensing and freezing up, take a deep breath and slowly breathe out
- prepare possible answers beforehand, but don't memorise them word for word because trying to remember them will create an additional stress
- 'go with the flow' and respond to what is happening at the interview.

Don't:
- play down your skills and experience
- sound too abrupt – this may happen if you feel shy and nervous
- get annoyed with your interviewer, even if you think the questions are silly or irrelevant.

Activity 5

When Rita Parks arrived at her interview for the post of electronic assembler, she felt very nervous. During the interview she had difficulty answering the questions, although she really knew the answers. There were long pauses while she tried to think about how to respond. Rita also forgot to tell the interviewer about the electronic assembly experience she already had. She did not get the job.

Give Rita some advice on interview practice.

_____

_____

_____

_____

_____

_____

_____

_____

You will find the feedback to this activity on page 22.

Types of question

There are several different types of question that you are likely to be asked at interviews. It is important to be able to recognise each type of question so that you know how to respond and how much information is expected.

Closed questions

This type of question is used to confirm information. For example: 'Are you still working?'

You do not need to give a long explanation in response to this type of question; usually just a 'yes' or 'no' answer is required.

Factual questions

This type of question is used to find out specific information. For example: 'When did you leave your last job?'

You should give a brief answer that includes all the necessary information, without going into too much detail.

Open questions

You will find that most questions will be of this type. For example: 'Can you tell me something about your current job?' 'What skills and experience do you have which make you a suitable candidate for this job?'

These questions need fuller answers. They give you an opportunity to demonstrate that you are the best candidate for the job.

Other points to be aware of

Try to suppress any mannerisms that you may have, such as biting your lip or tugging at your socks when trying to think of an answer. (It may help to ask a friend to point out any mannerisms, since we are not always aware of them ourselves.) These can divert attention from your answers and make you seem nervous and unsure of yourself.

Remember, if you feel you have done badly at an interview, it may not necessarily be your fault. Some interviewers, unfortunately, have a bad technique and ask ridiculous questions.

Activity 6

Write down whether each of the following is a closed, open or factual question.

(a) How many years did you work there for?

_____

(b) Could you tell me a little about what happened?

_____

(c) Is that your preferred option?

_____

(d) Why are you interested in the job?

_____

You will find the feedback to this activity on page 23.

Key Learning Points

☐ At the interview talk about your skills, experience and achievements that are relevant to the job.

☐ Try to relax and stay calm.

☐ Take time to think about your answers.

☐ Be friendly and pleasant to the interviewer, but don't be over-familiar.

☐ Respond to the different types of question in an appropriate way.

Section4 AFTER THE INTERVIEW

Reviewing what happened

If you were offered the job, well done! Try to remember what you think made your interview successful so that you can repeat your performance next time you apply for a job.

If you were not successful it is still important to think about your interview experience. You can learn from your mistakes so that next time you are better prepared. Some interviewers are happy to give you feedback; you could ask them to do this so that you can learn from their advice.

Answering questions

- Which questions did you find most difficult?
- Were there any questions that you could not answer?
- Which questions do you think you handled satisfactorily?
- With those questions which you found difficult, try to think why you found them difficult. Was it a lack of knowledge or skills, or just nerves?

For future job interviews make sure that you are better prepared in these areas.

Your appearance

- Did you feel confident about your appearance?
- Did you feel out of place because of the way you were dressed?
- Do you think you should have dressed more formally, or perhaps more casually?

These factors can affect the impression you give at an interview.

Other factors

- Were you late?
- Did you get lost or have difficulty finding your way?
- Do you think you made a fool of yourself in some way?

All of these things can stop you making a good impression and feeling confident.

Feedback from the organisation

Some organisations offer feedback to candidates after the interview. Always take advantage of this. If nothing is offered by the organisation, there is no harm in asking if they would be prepared to give you some feedback. Remember, however, that it is not the policy of some organisations to do this, so don't feel that it reflects on you personally if they decline to do so.

Activity 7

Think about interviews you have previously attended. What did you learn from your experience? Write your answer below.

_____
_____
_____
_____
_____
_____
_____
_____
_____
_____
_____
_____
_____
_____
_____
_____
_____
_____
_____
_____

FEEDBACK: Go through your answer with a friend or colleague and see if they can give you any advice.

DEVELOPING INTERVIEW SKILLS. LEARNING FOR WORK Series. © Workbase Training

Activity 8

Vikram attended an interview for a job as an operator on a busy production line. He was sure that he would get the job.

At the interview he was asked what he would do if the machine he was using broke down. He said he was good with machines so he would try to fix it. He was also asked about teamworking and said he would prefer to work alone.

Vikram found the chairs at the interview very comfortable. He sat back and almost fell asleep.

Vikram did not get the job. What can he do to ensure that he is more successful next time?

_____

_____

_____

_____

_____

_____

_____

_____

_____

_____

_____

_____

_____

_____

_____

You will find the feedback to this activity on page 23.

Key Learning Points

☐ After an interview, whether you are successful or not, you should think about what happened at the interview.

☐ Try to use your experience positively to help you prepare for your next interview.

☐ Ask the organisation if they provide feedback on candidates' performance.

Mini Project

When you next apply for a job prepare yourself in the following way.

Before the interview

- Complete your application form in rough first of all.
- Demonstrate in your answers that you meet any job specifications or criteria.
- Go through your answers with a friend or colleague, then write out the application form neatly.
- If you are asked to attend an interview, draft out answers to possible questions you may be asked.
- Find out as much about the organisation as you can.
- Work out how you are going to get to the interview.
- Think about what you are going to wear at the interview.

At the interview

- Try to make yourself relaxed.
- Demonstrate that you are the most suitable person for the job by giving information about your skills and experience.
- Think about each question carefully before answering.
- Refer to information that you have put on your application form and expand on it where appropriate.

After the interview

- Think about what happened at the interview.
- Think particularly about those questions you found most difficult.
- Use the checklist opposite to assess your performance.

Ask yourself the following questions.
Tick box as appropriate.

	Yes	No
Did you prepare well and were you able to ask relevant questions?		
Were you dressed appropriately and well groomed?		
Did you maintain eye contact with the interviewer?		
Did you give answers relevant to the questions asked and not ramble?		
Were you alert and attentive throughout the interview?		
Did you listen and respond well?		
Did you ask for questions not understood or unclear to be repeated?		
Did you sound confident?		
Did you provide appropriate information on your experience, strengths and achievements?		
Did you ask relevant questions?		
Did you take your time and pause for thought before answering?		
Did you sound interested and enthusiastic?		

If you answered 'no' to any of these questions, make sure you prepare yourself more thoroughly in these areas the next time you attend an interview.

FeedBack toActivities

FEEDBACK TO ACTIVITY 1

Below is a sample answer for the criteria which may be required for a learning assistant working with 4–7 year olds in a school.

1. Experience of working with under 10's in a paid or voluntary capacity.
2. Good reading and writing skills.
3. Driving licence, in order to transport equipment and materials.
4. Able to work flexibly and co-operatively with other members of the team.

FEEDBACK TO ACTIVITY 2

1. Read all the information carefully and get someone to help you read it if you are not a confident reader.
2. Complete the form in rough and then write it up neatly. Get someone else to check your grammar and spelling if you have problems.
3. Prepare yourself for the interview by reading through the form beforehand.

FEEDBACK TO ACTIVITY 4

1. Read the application form and other materials very carefully.
2. Be clear about what skills, knowledge and experience you have, particularly those which are relevant to the job.
3. Think about the requirements of the job and jot down answers to questions that you may be asked.
4. Pay special attention to your appearance.
5. Work out how you are going to get to the supermarket and allow plenty of time.

FEEDBACK TO ACTIVITY 5

1. Prepare for the interview in advance.
2. Try to relax and take deep breaths when you feel nervous.
3. Tell the interviewer about your skills and experience, even if you have already provided this information on your application form.
4. Try not to be too worried or nervous about the interview. After all, the worst thing that can happen is that you do not get the job.

DEVELOPING INTERVIEW SKILLS. LEARNING FOR WORK Series. © Workbase Training

FEEDBACK TO ACTIVITY 6

(a) Factual
(b) Open
(c) Closed
(d) Open

FEEDBACK TO ACTIVITY 8

1. He should ask for feedback from the organisation.
2. He should think more carefully about his answers. Mending the machine himself might be in breach of health and safety rules. Preferring to work alone is not appropriate for someone who is part of a busy production line, which relies on everyone's effort.
3. Slouching back in the chair and appearing sleepy does not create the right impression. Interviewers want candidates to be relaxed but they also expect them to appear alert and motivated.

Do you:
Get nervous when you have to attend an interview?
Panic when you have to complete a job application?
Want to know how to prepare for an interview?
Want to make a good impression during an interview?

If you answered 'Yes' to one or more of these questions, you will find that the activities and suggestions in this booklet will help you with the following:

- knowing how to prepare for an interview
- understanding what happens at interviews
- ensuring that you present yourself positively as the best person for the job
- reviewing how you performed and what improvements you can make.

WORKBASE TRAINING
Finchley House Business Centre
707 High Road
Finchley
London N12 0BT
Tel: 0208 492 0330
Fax: 0208 492 0405
e-mail:workbase@workbase.org.uk

INVESTOR IN PEOPLE

CAMPAIGN FOR LEARNING
19 Buckingham Street
London WC2N 6EF
Tel: 0207 930 1111
Fax:0207 930 1551
e-mail:campaign@cflearning.org.uk

INVESTOR IN PEOPLE

Workbase Training is the national specialist organisation for work force training and development. These booklets are based on work with over 20,000 employees within 120 organisations since 1980. Workbase is a not-for-profit charitable company, limited by guarantee, and is actively supported by the Confederation of British Industry, the Trades Union Congress and other unions.

The Campaign for Learning is a national charity seeking to create an appetite for learning in everyone. It has three main themes – Learning at Work, Family Learning and Learning to Learn – and it co-ordinates Learning at Work Day and Family Learning Weekend each year. The Campaign is supported by the DfEE, a wide range of businesses, local authorities, voluntary sector organisations, TECs and individuals.

Orders to:
SOUTHGATE PUBLISHERS LTD
The Square, Sandford, Crediton, Devon EX17 4LW
Tel: 01363 776888   Fax: 01363 776889
e-mail: info@southgatepublishers.co.uk

ISBN 1-85741-120-X

9 781857 411201